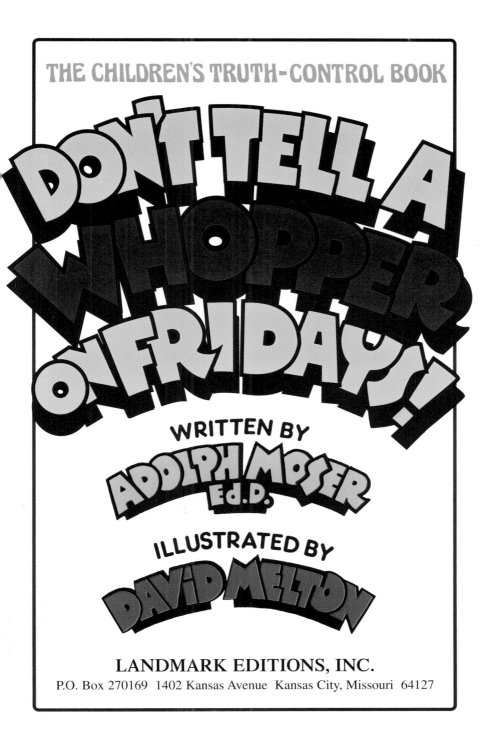

THE CHILDREN'S TRUTH-CONTROL BOOK

DON'T TELL A WHOPPER ON FRIDAYS!

WRITTEN BY

ADOLPH MOSER
Ed.D.

ILLUSTRATED BY

DAVID MELTON

LANDMARK EDITIONS, INC.

P.O. Box 270169 1402 Kansas Avenue Kansas City, Missouri 64127

Editorial Coordinator: Nancy R. Thatch
Creative Coordinator: David Melton
Computer Graphics Coordinator: Brian Hubbard

Printed in the United States of America

Landmark Editions, Inc.
P.O. Box 270169
1402 Kansas Avenue
Kansas City, Missouri 64127
(816) 241-4919

Dear Friend:

I wish I could tell you that I never have told a lie. But I can't do that because it wouldn't be true. The truth is — I *have* told lies. I told lies when I was a child. And I have told lies as an adult.

I was glad when people believed my lies, but I was never proud that I had lied to them. When people discovered I had lied about something, I always felt embarrassed and ashamed of myself.

When I finally realized that telling the truth was important, I decided to be a more truthful person. As I became a more truthful person, I soon had more friends, and I found that more people trusted me. That made me feel better about myself.

Because I believe that telling the truth is so important, I wrote this book just for you. I hope you enjoy it. And I hope the book will help you to become a more truthful person.

— Your friend,
Adolph Moser

It happens every day —

Some people open their mouths,
and they say things that are not true.

When they say untrue things,
they often tell themselves

they are not really telling lies.

They say they are just

"stretching the truth a little."

11

Sometimes
people tell
little lies.

Sometimes
they tell
medium-size lies.

WELL, YOU SEE IT WAS LIKE THIS —
AN OLD WOMAN WITH A GREEN FACE,
WHO WAS WEARING A BLACK DRESS
AND A TALL POINTED HAT, CAME IN
AND ASKED, *"WHERE IS DOROTHY?"*
BEFORE I COULD ANSWER, SHE SAW
MY PLATE, AND SHE SCREAMED,
"DON'T EAT THAT BROCCOLI!"
THEN SHE SCOOPED ALL OF THE
BROCCOLI OFF OF MY PLATE AND
THREW IT INTO THE GARBAGE, AND
SHE SAID, "SOME GIRL FROM KANSAS
TOOK MY SISTER'S RED SHOES!"

But sometimes people

tell WHOPPERS!

Not only do children tell WHOPPERS,

but adults do, too.

Almost everyone tells a lie
now and then —

big people, little people,
tall people, short people,

old people, young people,
  fat people, thin people.

Some people
don't lie
very often.

Other people lie a lot.
They tell one lie
after another, after another.

When some people lie,
they don't care
that it is wrong.

But when others lie,
they soon feel
ashamed of themselves.

Some people can look
at others, face to face,
and they can tell
an enormous WHOPPER.

But when others lie,
their faces get red,
and they have to turn
and look away.

When some people lie —
        their noses grow longer

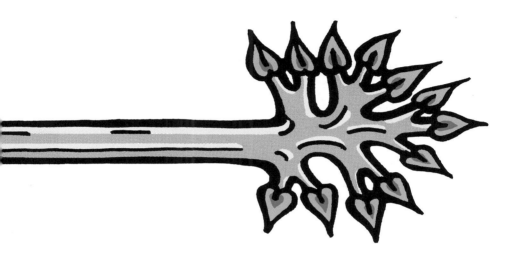

and longer, and longer, and longer!

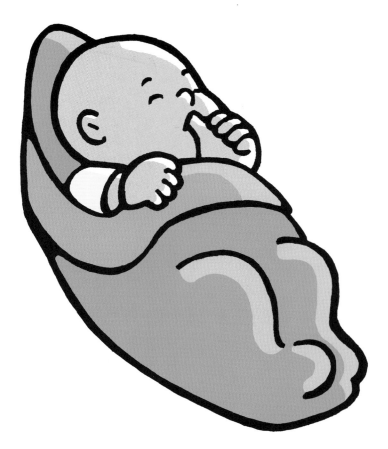

No one is born
knowing how
to tell lies.

But by two years of age,
most children have learned
how to tell them.

NO! NO! NO!
I CAN'T TELL!
I WON'T TELL!

Some people lie
because
they are afraid
to tell the truth.

HOW WOULD
YOU LIKE A
KARATE CHOP?

Some people lie
because
they don't want
to tell the truth.

people lie?

WHILE YOU WERE SHOPPING, AN EARTHQUAKE SHOOK YOUR VASE OFF OF THE TABLE. I WAS LUCKY THAT I WASN'T INJURED, TOO.

Other people lie because they don't want to admit that they have done something wrong.

31

When some people lie, they always

try to place the blame on others.

Some people think
lying will help them
get out of trouble.

But often,
telling lies gets people
into even more trouble.

When people
tell a lie,
they often
have to
tell other lies
to cover up
the first lie.
And they
dig themselves
deeper
and deeper,
and deeper
into a hole
of dishonesty.

When people lie,
they need to have
good memories,
so they can remember
what lies they have told
and to whom
they have told them.

If they can't remember
what lies they have told
and to whom
they have told them,
they often become confused
and are soon caught
in their lies.

Afraid of being caught
makes some people
very nervous.

They become so nervous,
they can't eat or
get to sleep at night.

41

If other people find out
you have lied to them,
they will stop believing

the things you tell them.
And they won't trust you
or respect you anymore.

If you want them
to trust you and
to respect you again,

then you must
apologize for lying
and tell them the truth.

Is it ever all right
to say things
that are not true?

Yes, it is.

Sometimes you may have to
"bend the truth,"
because you don't want
to hurt someone's feelings.

YOU are the only one
who can decide
whether or not

YOU will tell a lie
or YOU will tell the truth.
That choice is YOURS.

How do you stop
telling little lies
and BIG WHOPPERS?

50

You start by deciding
you *want to be*
a more honest person.

It might help
if you had
a reminder
that you could
carry with you
at all times.

YOUR THUMB
can be your reminder.

Look at
YOUR THUMB
and imagine
that it
can talk to you.

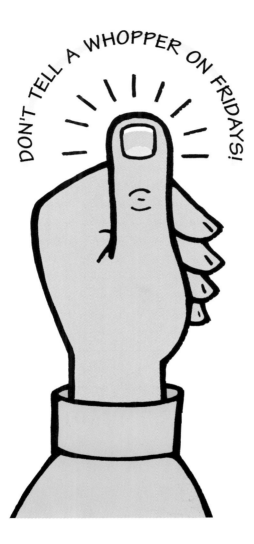

Imagine YOUR THUMB is saying,
"DON'T TELL A WHOPPER
ON FRIDAYS!"

On Friday,
if you start to tell a WHOPPER
— STOP! —

LOOK AT YOUR THUMB,
and it will remind you
TO TELL THE TRUTH.

After you
tell the truth
all day on Friday,
it will be easier

for you to tell the truth
on Saturday, and on Sunday,
and on all the other
days of the week.

Telling the truth is like ice skating —

the more you do it, the easier it becomes.

As you become
a more truthful person,
more people will trust you.
They will be very
pleased to know you.

And you will have
good reasons
to be proud of yourself.

AND THAT'S THE TRUTH!

If You Like FRIDAYS! — You'll Love MONDAYS! and TUESDAYS!

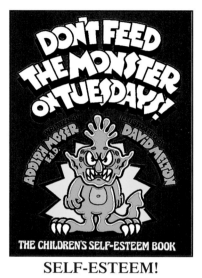

STRESS!

SELF-ESTEEM!

In these very informative handbooks for children, Dr. Adolph Moser offers practical approaches and effective techniques that can help young people deal with the problems of *Stress, Self-Esteem, Anger, and Grief.* The colorful illustrations by Dav Pilkey and David Melton project the perfect blend of broad humor and sensitivity.

For years, there has been a need for an entertaining, yet informative, stress-management book for children. Finally, it has occurred in the form of DON'T POP YOUR CORK ON MONDAYS!. I have seen no other book like it, and I enthusiastically recommend it to parents, teachers, clinicians and, of course, to children.

> — Theodore J. Tollefson, Ph.D., Clinical Psychologist

... read alouds should be as entertaining and informative for adults as they are for children. DON'T POP YOUR CORK ON MONDAYS! fits the rule to a tee. Adolph Moser has given parents and children an enjoyable way to learn about their own behavior. I love it!

> — William F. Russell, author of
> CLASSICS TO READ ALOUD TO YOUR CHILDREN

Every school year should start with having students read DON'T FEED THE MONSTER ON TUESDAYS!. I can't think of a better beginning for children. Try it! You'll like it!

> — Bonnie G. Molloy, Educator, Parent, Nurturing Grandparent

and WEDNESDAYS! and THURSDAYS!

ANGER!   GRIEF!

The Emotional Impact Series Explains and Informs! These wonderful books are invaluable resources for clinicians, teachers, parents, and everyone else who works with children.

> — Judy S. Freedman, LCSW, Creator of STRESS*ED,
> School Social Worker, and Parent

I highly recommend DON'T FEED THE MONSTER ON TUESDAYS! for parents and teachers who are genuinely interested in helping their children build good self-esteem. Make a child feel special by reading this book to him. It will be fun!

> — Robert S. Craig, Ed.D., Psychologist and Clinic Director

DON'T RANT & RAVE ON WEDNESDAYS! is a delightful addition to Dr. Moser's Emotional Impact Series for children! With the right combination of information and humor, he clearly defines the complicated emotion of anger and offers workable suggestions to help youngsters better control their anger and their behavior.

> — Sue Clarke, Coordinator of Gifted Programs

In DON'T RANT & RAVE ON WEDNESDAYS!, Dr. Moser presents clinically accurate, helpful lessons in life to young people in a most entertaining manner. The examples are well chosen, and the engaging illustrations carry the text into the hearts and minds of children of all ages.

> — Dr. Debra E. Taylor-McGee, HSPP, Licensed Psychologist

Adolph Moser — author

Dr. Adolph Moser is a licensed clinical psychologist in private practice, specializing in bio-behavioral and cognitive approaches to stress-related syndromes. He is founder of the Center for Human Potential, a nonprofit organization with holistic focus on preventing acute onsets of stress in children. While Chief Psychologist at the Indiana Youth Center, he implemented a biofeedback laboratory and directed a nine-year research project on the effects of relaxation techniques in the treatment of stress disorders. That study culminated in the development of the nationally distributed stress-management program, entitled SYSTEMATIC RELAXATION TRAINING.

Raised in Indiana, Dr. Moser is a graduate of the universities of Purdue and Indiana. He is certified in biofeedback and is a Diplomate Stressologist. He is also a Diplomate in Behavioral Medicine and Psychotherapy, and a Fellow and Diplomate in Medical Psychotherapy. Dr. Moser is listed in WHO'S WHO IN THE BIO-BEHAVIORAL SCIENCES. In 1987, he received the "Outstanding Psychologist of the Year" award from the National Prisoners' Rights Union.

After becoming parents, Dr. Moser and his wife, Dr. Kathryn Moser, who is also a psychologist, expanded their professional practices to include normal problems of childhood and parenting. They co-authored a newspaper column, "Positive Parenting," for ten years.

Dr. Moser is the father of three children, spanning pre-school to adolescence, which explains his perennial interest in stress and anger management.

All of Dr. Moser's books in his EMOTIONAL IMPACT SERIES have received outstanding reviews and enthusiastic acceptance from children, parents, counselors, and educators nationwide.

David Melton — illustrator

David Melton is one of the most versatile and prolific talents on the literary and art scenes today. His literary works span the gamut of factual prose, newsreporting, analytical essays, magazine articles, features, short stories, and poetry and novels in both the adult and juvenile fields. In the past thirty years, twenty-one of his books have been published. Several of them have been translated into a number of foreign languages.

Mr. Melton has illustrated ten of his own books and seven by other authors. Many of his drawings and paintings have been reproduced as fine art prints, posters, puzzles, calendars, book jackets, record covers, mobiles, and note cards, and have been featured in national publications.

Since a number of Mr. Melton's books are enjoyed by children, he has visited hundreds of schools throughout the country as a principal speaker in Young Authors' Days, Author-in-Residence Programs, and Children's Literature Festivals. Each year, he also conducts his WRITTEN & ILLUSTRATED BY... WORKSHOPS for students and educators, effectively teaching participants to write and illustrate original books.

Mr. Melton's teacher's manual, WRITTEN & ILLUSTRATED BY..., has been highly acclaimed and has been used by thousands of teachers nationwide to instruct their students in how to write and illustrate amazing books. To provide opportunities for the original books by students to be published, in association with Landmark Editions, Inc., in 1986, Mr. Melton initiated THE NATIONAL WRITTEN & ILLUSTRATED BY... AWARDS CONTEST FOR STUDENTS.

Mr. Melton is also a book publisher. During the last fourteen years, as Creative Coordinator at Landmark Editions, he has supervised the publication of more than fifty books by other authors and illustrators.